Jahmo and the Giant

By

C.D. Thomas

ISBN: 1-4033-4166-4 (e-book)
ISBN: 1-4033-4167-2 (Paperback)

This book is printed on acid free paper.

1stBooks – rev. 09/18/02

JAHMO

Jahmo was the son of a Great King who lived long ago in a beautiful land in Africa. Jahmo was handsome and brave, with a kind heart and was well liked by his people. He had strong shoulders and an easy smile for everyone. He was smart, strong and swift footed. In fact it was had to find fault in the young prince at all, except for the fact that he seemed to be a little smaller than most of the other

boys. Well, he was smaller than all

the other boys it was true, Jahmo was

short in stature but it didn't seem to

bother anyone least of all Jahmo.

Jahmo's father was a Mighty King.

He stood tall and proud, walked with

majestic slow strides and spoke in a

deep low commanding voice. Jahmo,

he would say, you are becoming a

man now and my beard grows white like snowcaps on the Mountain. Your thoughts must now turn to being ruler of our people and taking a bride for your Queen. There are dozens of beautiful maidens who would be thrilled at the opportunity to have you ask for their hand. Jahmo stood quietly then finally he spoke, "Father, he said, it is true, the young women of our village are very beautiful indeed."

"I have been aware of this fact for

quite some time." The King smiled

JAHMO AND OTHER BOYS

proudly.   But…Jahmo continued, "when I look at the beautiful girls of our village I do not feel in my heart what I see in your eyes when you look at my mother, the Queen.   It makes me smile so, when I see you looking at each other in that special way.

Er…Ahhun…Well I…The King stammered.   The King then smiled

and sighed. "Truly you are wise my son you will be a Great King, far greater and wiser than I, no doubt." The King said as he placed his hands on Jahmo's shoulders. Jahmo grinned so hard his cheeks began to hurt. Jahmo loved his father very much.

Jahmo thought to himself, this would be the perfect time to tell his father of how he longed for adventure. "Father", he asked, "did you have many adventures when you were my age?" "Why yes my son," the King answered, "many, many adventures." "Why do you ask the King suddenly inquired." "Because that is my heart's desire, great one, that is where my thoughts turn." "To have one, just one great adventure." "Oh Jahmo," the King moaned, as his eyes rolled back, "you can't be serious my son." "Yes Sire after all you just said you had many, many adventures when

MAIDENS OF VILLAGE

you were my age." "Let us speak no further of this nonsense," the King commanded sternly. I will not speak of this anymore, Jahmo muttered weakly, for now he thought to himself.

The next day a messenger from a far off land came to Jahmo's village. "I come with a message from King Amaal the Great." The messenger proclaimed, "Let all the Great Nations of all the land send one of Royal blood, one Prince true and brave, a Prince who would face the evil Giant Booli and win the hand of the beautiful Princess Tomu. (An adventure Jahmo thought aloud). "Now wait a moment the King said firmly." "Father please let me go," Jahmo begged. The King cut his eyes sharply at the messenger, who quickly retreated from the village.

Very well the King said but first your adventure starts here. You must go see the ancient one, Old Pa, the Elder. That will begin your adventure.

Old Pa was said to be hundreds of years old. Even the oldest villagers remembered him as ancient when

they were small children. Old Pa

lived in a small hut just outside the

village. He was withered and

shriveled like dried fruit. He walked

KING AND QUEEN

JAHMO'S PARENTS

about slowly with a twisted little stick. He was said to know everything about everything.

The young Prince journeyed to the outskirts of the village to see the ancient wise Old Pa. At the suggestion of his Father, Jahmo brought a basket of fruit, and a pail of fresh milk as a friendly gesture. The little old man stood in a clearing almost as if he were waiting on Jahmo. "Come closer," the old man murmured in a voice like dried wood on a fire. "Old Pa, I am Jahmo, son of the King, I have come to seek your counsel, please accept this basket of fruit and fresh milk as a humble offering to your wisdom." "My, but you're a mannerable boy", the old man muttered with a smile. "Good,

Good the King has taught you well, sit down here before me boy." Jahmo sat down quickly in front of the old man. "Yes, yes, yes," the old man began, "I see you have it." "Have what," Jahmo asked. "Be silent." The old man snapped. "Young Prince," Old Pa continued, "even though sight has left my eyes, my old tired eyes. I see you have the Gift.

"Gift?" said Jahmo. "You are talking

again boy," Old Pa snapped again.

WISE OLD PA

"Yes boy, the gift, Natures Gift. Why do you think it is that you run fast as you do and hold your own and even surpass young men nearly twice your size. You are special and not because you are the son of the King, No, No" he said. "You have the gift and no idea how to use it."

The old man shuffled closer. "Close your eyes little prince," Old Pa said, placing his withered old hand over Jahmo's face. "Be still, be silent and listen, listen for the first time in your life, to the sound of Natures Heart." Jahmo was completely still and silent. He heard nothing, nothing at all. "I don't hear anything Old Pa," Jahmo said with a whimper. "Let me help you then boy, listen now," the old man stopped suddenly. "Now,

now hear it." "Hear the wind as it sings beneath the wings of the Eagle, the dust beneath the strides of the Panther as he chases his prey. Listen boy, as the Earth trembles at the footsteps of the elephant as he walks along the waterfall. Close your eyes, be silent and hear these things boy."

Suddenly, slowly Jahmo could hear all the things the old man had said.

He could hear the wings of a bee buzzing a half a mile away. He could hear the heartbeat of the mighty Lion as he lay panting under a shady tree in the Plains. "I hear Old Pa," Jahmo grinned. "This is your gift young Prince from the Creator of all things under the sky and above it. You may call on all of Natures Creatures, great and small and they will do your bidding. You are a very smart boy. Remember your gift and your wits and you can over come any obstacle before you even a giant one." The old man smiled a big toothless smile and said "Thank you for the fruit and milk, now leave me", as he shuffled into his little hut.

Jahmo was ready to begin his journey to the far off Kingdom. He kissed his Mother and Father good

bye and waived fair well to his friends

and the people of the village. After

he had traveled many days he came

upon a Great City at the foot of a

mountain by a winding river. This

was the City of King Amaal and his

daughter, the Princess. As Jahmo

entered the city he came upon other

young men from all over. Some from

far off lands further than even Jahmo

had journeyed. In all, twenty brave

young, and not so young, princes had

come to face the Giant, Booli.

They stood in the square, some

garbed in fine robes and jewels.

OTHERLAND PRINCE

OTHERLAND PRINCE

Some had servants who waited on them hand and foot. Some boasted of their brave deeds. Some were pampered, puffed peacocks, Jahmo thought to himself. All of course were taller than Jahmo.

As the young men stood in a square a low rumbling began in the distance. It began to grow as a huge dust cloud approached the Kingdom. The

OTHERLAND PRINCE

rumbling grew louder and louder from within the swirl of dust that grew bigger and bigger. It traveled straight up the road right into the center of the city, till it thundered like stampeding elephants. From the middle emerged a chariot pulled by two rhinoceros black as night with blood red eyes. The chariot was driven by Booli the Giant himself.

The Chariot stopped just short of the young men in the square, kicking dirt into their faces. As they coughed and started to slowly step back. The Giant stepped from the Chariot with a scowl of disdain for all gathered in the square. The Giant stood tall as a tree. he had long pointed ears like a Jackal and colorless eyes, that seemed to look right though you. He had

huge

EVIL GIANT

Craig Thomas

BOOLI THE GIANT AND JAHMO

snarling teeth like an angry tiger and

his arms bulged like great serpents

crawled beneath his skin and his heart

was cold as stone. No man had ever

dared stand against him.

Booli had long plagued the

Kingdom, blocking the river flow

stealing cattle small herds all at once

and terrorizing the people at every

opportunity. He had pledged to

continue doing so until the Princess agreed to marry him. He had given her one year to decide and her time was nearly up.

As the Giant stood before the men in the square, more than a few could not hide their fear. The bravest of them stood fast choking down their fear including Jahmo, who was still more that a little nervous. Yet, he stood firm preparing for the worst.

Finally the Giant spoke, "So," he

bellowed, one Prince fainted dead

away and was dragged off by his

servants. "You are the mice who

would dare to stand against me!" "I

say to you little mice," he continued,

"to face me is to face your doom."

"This is your only warning." He

smirked and spat at the feet of the

young men gathered in the square. And with that he mounted his chariot laughing and sped away.

Suddenly several brave Princes began packing their belongings. Several more hurriedly gathered their servants and wagons and whatever means of transportation they were utilizing and began a hasty retreat to their Homelands. When the

FACING THE GIANT

commotion ended only Jahmo and four others were left.

King Amaal and Princess Tomu greeted the remaining brave young men. "Gentlemen you do us a great honor," said King Amaal. "This is my daughter princess Tomu, which

TOMU

means sweetness." She was breath takingly beautiful and moved with an elegant sway like the treetops dancing from the whisper of a cool breeze in the evening. The Princess spoke, "there is one test you must first pass honorable sirs. The one of you who can beat me in a foot race will be my Champion." The men in the square laughed all except Jahmo. He could

OTHERLAND PRINCE

not take his eyes off the beautiful girl before him. He had never seen a girl as beautiful as the Princess. "Come little flower let me be first so these others may start their long journeys home," said a strapping young Prince from the south. "Let us begin. Are you ready my dear," he said. "Yes," replied the Princess. "GO!" He

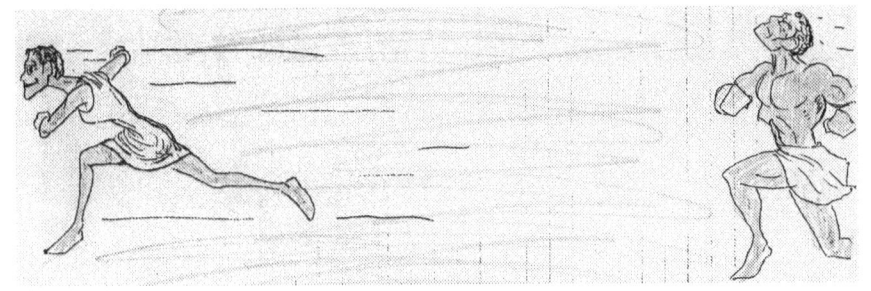

PRINCESS OUTRUNS THEM ALL

shouted, as he laughed running in long full strides.

But to his surprise and the surprise of the others, Tomu practically flew past him almost effortlessly. "Wait! Wait!" he cried, "I...I wasn't ready." he exclaimed. "Let us go again." And again she strode past him and the others. Jahmo was already stricken with the Princess but when he saw her run he was even more stunned.

The Princess could run faster then any maiden he'd' ever seen or any man for that matter. She runs like a jungle cat said one Prince as she breezed past him. She even looked back and laughed at a few young men as she past them. As Jahmo watched her run his heart pounded in his chest as though it would leap from his body. He felt dizzy and woozy in a silly happy sort of way. Jahmo had never felt this way before.

This must be it, he thought to himself, this must be what Jahmo saw in his Father's eyes when he looked at his Mother. This must be love, he thought. Oh my, he said to himself. Jahmo was in love and he knew right then, there was nothing he wouldn't do for her. No challenge he wouldn't accept and no Giant he wouldn't face.

"Are you ready young man?" a voice said to Jahmo, snapping him out of his trance. "It's your turn." The remaining men laughed, if we could not beat her speed what chance does this pygmy stand. Why you arrogant peacock Jahmo grumbled. The Pygmy Prince deserves his chance, too! Commanded King Amaal. "I am not a pygmy," shouted Jahmo. "I am Jahmo! The Princess looked at him and smiled. "You will have your turn just the same Prince Jahmo, are you ready." "Um...uh...no sweet Princess," he replied. "I don't understand," she said. "Sweet Princess," he began, I wish to give you an opportunity to rest yourself. I will race you tomorrow at dawn." "Very well then tomorrow at dawn scoffed the King."

Jahmo knew he could not out run the Princess even as fast as he was. A jungle cat he remembered, Jahmo had an idea. When the Kingdom was asleep Jahmo rose and ran far into the Jungle. There he could find one who would help him.

He came upon her in a deep brushy thicket. "Cheetah great huntress," he called to her. "Hear me I need your help. The sleek cat walked up to him and sat before him, "I will listen," she said. Jahmo didn't have time to be amazed, he explained his plight to her.　"Oh, I despise that Giant myself," she said.　"I will help you little Prince."　"I will give you my speed from dawn till the sun is high,

OTHERLAND PRINCE

CHEETAH THE HUNTRESS

then it will return to me." "Thank you Huntress," Jahmo said. "Remember, Jahmo, I am a Cheetah, I run fast but not very far, I tire quickly." "Keep your race with the Princess short." "Now look into my eyes." Jahmo looked into her deep green eyes. "See what I see man Prince, feel what I feel." Slowly Jahmo felt his muscles twitch and tighten, it was like before with Old Pa only now more intense, the Huntress fell into a deep sleep.

Jahmo made his way back to the Kingdom it was nearly dawn. The Princess and the others were already waiting for him by time he returned. "Sorry I'm late," he apologized. "He actually decided to show up," teased one Prince who still remained. "Yes we thought you'd sneak away not wanting to embarrass yourself." "I knew he would come," said the Princess smiling at Jahmo. Jahmo looked at her and couldn't help but smile too. "You are the last of my would be Champions and I thank you for your bravery, but I warn you I will run against you as fast as I can, you understand don't you."

The Princess didn't think Jahmo had a chance. No one did. The remaining Princes began to wager on how badly he would loose to the Princess, twenty lengths shouted one thirty said another. "Don't worry Princess," Jahmo said, "I understand and I want you to do your best."

"Get Ready!" said King Amaal, Get Set…Go!" Jahmo and Tomu both took off. It was incredible, to the surprise of all, including Tomu. Not only was the little Prince keeping up, he was beginning to pass Tomu. The Princess couldn't believe it, this had never happened before. She frowned and ran faster and faster, but unlike the many times before Jahmo was not behind her, he was even further in front of her. She clenched her fists tighter, gritted her teeth and ran faster and faster, faster than she'd ever run before. She began to close in on Jahmo, getting closer and closer.

Jahmo remembered what the huntress had told him, he felt himself growing tired and slower and slower. But he couldn't give up he had to win, he just had to. They both crossed the finish line where King Amaal stood.

They both fell to the ground and looked at him. It was close he said, but the Prince of Pygmy's wins, he is my daughter's Champion against Booli, The Giant."

"You may start your long journeys to your homelands," Jahmo said to the other Princes as he walked by. As the

THE RACE

other young men left, the Princess

approached Jahmo. "How were you

able to beat me, no man has ever

beaten me before," she asked. "I have

a special gift," Jahmo replied. "What

kind of gift my Champion," Tomu asked. "I will tell you when we are wed sweetness," said Jahmo. The Princess blushed, "Very well, tomorrow you will meet the Giant."

The next day the Giant met with the King Amaal, Jahmo, and the Princess. When he saw Jahmo, he laughed. "Tomu," he roared laughing, "just when I thought you didn't care to be my bride." "But if this mosquito is the champion you've chosen, you must find me much more becoming than I could have imagined. That is good for I find you quite pleasant to

the eye too!" Booli looked at Tomu with a evil smile that chilled her to the bone. "Come let me quickly swat this gnat and we can be wed right away."

The Giant began to lumber toward Jahmo looming over him. Jahmo sighed a bored unimpressed sigh. Then suddenly Jahmo frowned and yelled up to Booli, "Hold there

JAHMO

Giant!"   "I was tested for my worthiness to face you, now you must be tested to prove you are worthy to face me!"   "My Worthiness," the Giant growled. "Why you puny little dirt mite how dare you I'll..."   "Be silent," Jahmo snapped. "you must pass   the...Ah...ten   trails   of worthiness before you have the honor of me peeling you like a grape, before you have the privilege of me flaying your lumbering carcass." "I'll break you into pieces," rumbled the Giant. "Booli!" cried the Princess, stopping the Giant just before he struck. "I would ask you to submit to Prince Jahmos traditional rituals, after all he did pass our test of worthiness," "I will not!" exclaimed the Giant. "I am the one who is being challenged, I have waited for nearly a year." "And you will wait even longer Giant, until this matter is settled," said King Amaal. "Don't tempt me Little King," snarled Booli." "Booli," the Princess said, batting her eyes at the Giant, "please for me," she said forcing a smile.

The Giant stood quiet for a long moment. "Princess Sweetness," the

Giant said struggling to maintain his composure, "surely you can't expect me to subject myself to ten, ten trails of worthiness for this dirt mite after all sweet one only one test was required of him." "I will perform one feat also." "Yes, I will submit to one test for you my little sweetness, Jahmo frowned again. One test for one test quipped the Giant in a diplomatic voice." "Three tests," the Princess proclaimed with finality. "Very well then little dirt mite, let us begin, what challenge do you have for me?" "What tests await Booli that he may prove his worthiness, come with it what do you have?"

"What test do I have? " Jahmo repeated unsuredly. He had no idea, there were no trials of worthiness.

"Yes, yes you annoying little flea." Jahmo desperately tried to think of something.   "Sweet   Princess tomorrow at dawn we will begin the proof of our worthiness," Jahmo said with confidence.   "Princess must I continue this humiliating charade, I planned to meet whatever feeble challenge the little mud rat had to offer, slay him and for us to be married by the end of the day,"

whined the Giant. Tomu, princess

sweetness," Jahmo again interrupted,

"one test per day will be

required..."What, that'll take three

days!" The Giant shouted, cutting

Jahmo off in mid sentence. "We will

begin tomorrow at dawn, at the end of

three days, one of you will have the

hand of the princess," commanded

King Amaal. "This is the final word on the matter!" "Very well then dwarf, dawn it is." With that the giant was gone.

"Oh Jahmo," the princess said with a worried voice. "I fear for you." "I know you have a special gift." "Well yes," said Jahmo. "Yes, and when the time comes, I want you to use the gift and run away as fast as you can," she said. "I don't want the Giant to harm you." It won't be so bad being the wife of a cruel, mean, evil, ugly Giant." I'm sure I'll get used to it." "You won't have to sweetness, I swear it," Jahmo said, grasping the young girl's hand.

"You are so brave, my handsome little champion," Tomu said planting the softest whisper of a kiss on

Jahmo's forehead as she left. "She kissed me," Jahmo thought aloud. Smiling a woozy dreamy eyed smile. "And she said I was handsome." "After the three rituals of worthiness and I've vanquished the Giant we can be wed." "That is as soon as I think of three tests and figure out some way to defeat him," he rippled, snapping out of his trance. "What will I do?"

As night fell upon the Kingdom, Jahmo sat alone by the river again thinking aloud. "Birds in the air…um no." "Fish in the water…no, no." I like fish," said a weary sounding voice. It was an old green turtle, trodding slowly up from the water. "Hello, old brother turtle, said Jahmo.

Jahmo had an idea. "Tell me brother turtle do you know the river well?"

"That I do youngster after all it is my home." "Would you by chance know of any treasure in the river." "What is treasure?" asked the old turtle. You know the shiny stones men love so much. Oh yes, I know of treasure. "Oh, Yes! I know of lots of treasure." "Why do you men love treasure so much anyway?"   "I really can't say old brother, but love it they do." "Can you show me where the shiny rocks are?"   "Of course little man Prince...Oh, no wait no I can not." "The place where this treasure is, is infested with crocodiles."   "Good, good that's even better," smiled Jahmo.   The old turtle looked at Jahmo curiously and for a brief moment he reminded Jahmo of the ancient Old Pa. "I am a slow one little Prince I do not understand."

"You are slow indeed," laughed Jahmo. The turtle laughed too.

I am slow on land it is true, but in the water I float with the grace of the Eagle flying over the mountain." "Eagle?" said Jahmo. "Yes, boy!" the turtle said. Jahmo had another idea.

You are quicker than you know," Jahmo began to explain. He and the old turtle talked for hours, until it was nearly dawn.

At dawn Jahmo met with King Amaal, Princess and the Giant. "The first test is as follows," announced Jahmo. "At the bottom of the river lies golden treasure." "Whoever swims to the bottom and retrieves the most gold is the winner of the first challenge." But first you must get past a nest of hungry crocodiles."

"This is ridiculous," said the Giant. How could the dirt mite know there is gold at the bottom of the river." "This is obviously and attempt to have the crocodiles attack me." "Nice try dwarf but no beast or man can hurt Booli the Giant." "I see right through your feeble plan, you treacherous little snake, do you think I'm stupid?"

"Why yes I Booli, I do," snapped Jahmo. "You insolent little whelp I'll snap you in two!" the Giant stopped suddenly. "Very well let us begin," he said slyly, with a sinister grin, "but you will, of course, go first." "But of course," said Jahmo. "That was my intention all along." "Wait here,"

Jahmo said, to a stunned giant.

Jahmo walked down to the edge of the river where dozens of crocodiles wallowed in the shallow water.

"Hello their my brothers, I am Jahmo," he called to them. "You are no brother of mine, manling, come closer so you may be our lunch,

CROCODILE

Uhm…" "I would like to ask a small favor of you my friends." Would you consider allowing me to swim through your home to retrieve the yellow stones at the bottom." "Certainly, little manling come into

the water with us," the largest of the

crocs replied. "Come closer let us be

friends," he laughed. "What's the

matter little mud rat?" the Giant

MOTHER HIPPO

called to Jahmo. "What are you doing there?" Just then a huge mother hippopotamus swam up behind the crocodiles with old brother turtle close behind. "Let the manling pass, unless you want to deal with me," she snorted.

The crocodiles hissed and snapped at the waters but obediently moved back just the same. Booli looked on curiously, he still could not make out what Jahmo was doing. "Old brother turtle," said Jahmo, "lend me your grace in the water." "Certainly little Prince if it makes things easier for you and your human lungs." Jahmo looked over his shoulders at the Giant who was now walking closer. Jahmo raised both fists into the air and shouted. "I am the mighty Prince

Jahmo you crocodiles will move back or feel my wrath!" "You too Hippo," he shouted. "Humph!" said mother Hippo. The Giant looked on in disbelief. "Sorry mother," he whispered to her. The old turtle snapped his jaws around the end of the Hippo's tail and fell into a deep sleep, and was pulled by the mother Hippo towing him around as he slept.

Jahmo dove into the water, deeper

and deeper he swam, his arms and

legs feeling so powerful as he stroked

JAHMO DIVES FOR GOLD

effortlessly through the water. He knew if not for the old turtle, his lungs would be burning for air. When Jahmo reached the bottom of the river there were chunks of gold and gold nuggets right where old brother turtle had said. Jahmo gathered as much as he could carry and swam back to the surface. "Thank you brother turtle," Jahmo said as the turtle awoke from his sleep. "Thank you mother,' Jahmo whispered. "Humph!" she said as she swam away smiling.

The Giant's jaw dropped when Jahmo plopped the gold at his feet. "For you King Amaal," said Jahmo. "Well Giant if you can retrieve more gold than I, you win, in fact I will concede the entire challenge to you and the Princess is yours." "I am no fool," fumed the Giant. "It's a trick, sorcery!" "It's no sorcery," said Jahmo, "of course if you are afraid just say so." "Booli afraid of a few tiny crocodiles." The Giant stormed to the edge of the river. "All right you slimy worthless lizards, hear me, I am Booli the Giant," he shouted, "let all tremble before me, all men and all beasts." "Now I command let me pass!" The Giant then jumped into the river. The crocodiles immediately swarmed the Giant. The water rippled with huge waves as Booli flailed and thrashed against the frenzy of gnashing teeth and whipping thick tails. Then the water grew silent and still with no movement. "Oh no I've killed the lumbering oaf," said Jahmo. Just then the water exploded with a tremendous splash and the Giant went catapulting straight into the air and out of the water. Jahmo sighed with relief. Booli landed on the shore battered bruised and aching,

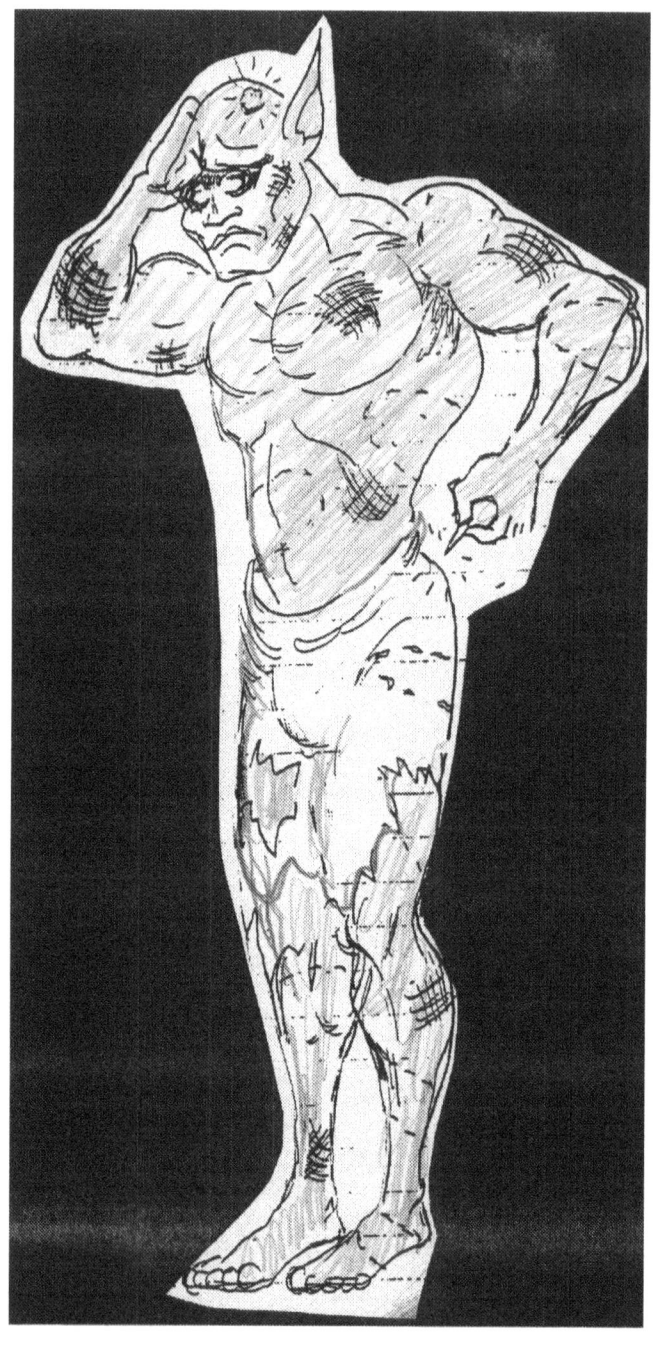

plucking a large crocodile tooth from his backside.

"The second test is tomorrow at dawn," he shouted to the Giant as he staggered away. "I'll try not to be so hard on you," the little Prince grinned.

Tomu ran to Jahmo and threw her arms around him." You were incredible she shouted jumping up and down." "I too am over whelmed," beamed King Amaal. "You'll be a fine son in law." "How did you do it?" asked King Amaal. "I have a special gift," replied Jahmo. "That you do boy, that you do," said the King.

"Sweetness," Jahmo said to the Princess, if you don't mind tomorrow I would like to face the Giant alone. She and King Amaal agreed. The next day Jahmo met the Giant as the sun arose. "Today's test is this Giant, we will both scale this nearby mountain." "Whoever reaches the top first wins." "I am ready small one," said the Giant. He seemed to take Jahmo more seriously. "Then let us proceed huge one." The Giant leapt into the air, climbing up the mountain in staggering bounds. Up he climbed frequently looking back down at Jahmo who just stood on the ground not moving at all, smiling up at him.

The Giant climbed so high until he could no longer see the little Prince for the cover of clouds near the mountain top. Booli was certain he would win this contest.

Jahmo then closed his eyes and called out, "Oh great Eagle, King of the sky." "I Prince Jahmo call upon you I need your help." The sky king heard Jahmo's call and down from the heavens he came. "What is it I can do for you, Prince of the ground," he asked. "Lift me up to the top of this mountain." The mighty Eagle swooped down and grasped Jahmo gently in his razor sharp talons, up, up he flew higher and higher up the other

side of the mountain where Booli

could not see them.   They sailed

through the clouds and to the very top

of the snow capped mountain. "You will take me back down, won't you?" asked Jahmo. He'd never been to the top of a mountain before and was unnerved by the height. Of course little ground prince, are you ready now?" "Oh no, give me a moment please, I'm meeting someone here shortly." The giant bird turned his head sideways and looked at Jahmo curiously. "Very well, I will circle the mountain until you are ready. You have only to call and I will return." The majestic eagle then flew off.

The weary giant soon made his way to the top of the mountain, huffing and wheezing and nearly out of strength, only to find Jahmo lounging at the mountain's peak. "Ho there giant!" Jahmo called smiling and waving. "It's cold up here isn't it?" the little prince said with a grin. The weakened giant stood in disbelieve, "how, how did you beat me, I don't believe it, the giant said shaking his head. You were still at the bottom, I watched you till you were a speck behind the clouds its impossible." "Well believe it, it is possible, I thought I'd give you a sporting chance, I even climbed up this more difficult side of the mountain for you, Jahmo said pointing the other side of the mountain." "Would you like to see who can reach the bottom first?"

"You will little mouse, when I throw you off!" Booli snarled. "I'd advise against it," Jahmo said bravely. "You're far too weak right now, while

I'm not winded at all. You'd be no match for me, besides we both gave our word to the Princess." You'll get your chance soon enough and I'll get mine," Jahmo said fiercely with a sudden cold stare. The Giant stood quiet with a puzzled look on his face. It was true, the little Prince did not seem the least bit tired and the Giant was nearly spent.

"Alright then princeling, back down then," Booli said, leaping down the mountainside in incredible bounds. "Sky King!" Jahmo called, "Quickly take me down." "Afraid of heights are you?" asked the mighty Eagle as he appeared as though out of the sun. "Please great eagle hurry," said Jahmo. "All right," the bird said. "Don't get your tail feathers in an uproar." The eagle again swooped up the little Prince and safely flew him to the ground. "Thank you brother eagle," said Jahmo to the great bird. "You are welcome little prince," he replied, and soared away in to the sky.

Soon afterward the Giant came tumbling down the mountainside, rolling to the ground exhausted. The Giant lay on the ground gasping for

breath holding his chest. "Are you all

right?" Jahmo asked genuinely

concerned. The Giant tried to speak

but could not. Let me fetch you some

water," Jahmo said. Running to a

nearby well and quickly returning

with a full pail for the drained Giant.

The Giant drank all the water. "Are you all right," Jahmo asked again. "Will you be able to go on with the third trial tomorrow or do you wish to stop now. The Giant flung the bucket to the ground angrily, of course I'm all right he wheezed furiously.

"How very rude!" Jahmo frowned, "all right then, we will continue with the third trial tomorrow." "Then I will slay you." "I'll try to make it as quick and painless as possible," Prince Jahmo said politely. "You look terrible why don't you just rest right there, your going to need all your strength tomorrow." ""Goodbye," Jahmo said waving and walked back into the kingdom.

The next day Jahmo met the Giant at the foot of the mountain. Booli had fallen asleep right where Jahmo had left him. "Wake up Giant!" Jahmo shouted into Booli's long pointed ear. Booli stirred and shook achingly he could hardly move he was so weak. Well this is the third and final test the Prince said. It is a test of strength and endurance. "Oh wonderful," Booli groaned quietly to himself.

There are three great stones there at the base of the mountain" Jahmo pointed. "Each of us will choose a stone and push it all the way to the other side of the mountain." "Who ever reaches the other side first is the winner." The stones were huge, all bigger even than the Giant. Booli was unsure if he had enough strength to perform such a feat, even if he weren't in such a weakened state.

"I agree," Booli said hesitantly, "I choose this one," he said picking the smallest of the tremendous stones.

GIANT PUSHES GREAT STONE

Huffing and straining with what was

left of his strength he began to push,

barely moving the stone at all. The

little prince just stood and watched

smiling. The Giant stopped abruptly, "Why aren't you pushing a stone," he questioned. "Is this a trick, are you trying to make a fool of me?" "Oh no, great one, I'm just trying to give you a fair head start as always, while I decide which of the great stones I push." "Besides, you do a fine job of making a fool of yourself without any help from me." "Push both remaining stones, if you want to be so fair to me!" "That's a good idea," said Jahmo. "I will push both stones Giant." "We will see who is the fool," Booli grumbled pushing now even harder, slowly moving the huge stone.

Prince Jahmo waited till Booli was nearly out of sight rounding the

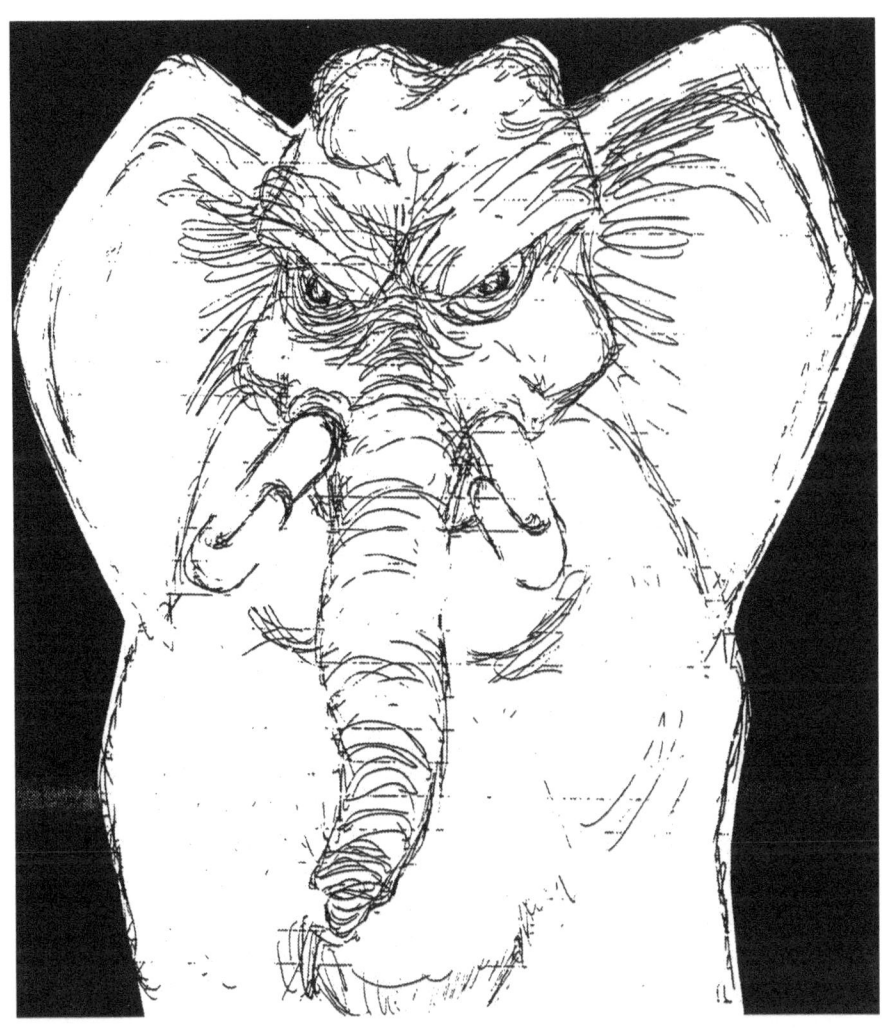

corner of the mountain. "Mighty

elephant he called, please come to my

aid." Out of the trees emerged a hulking bull elephant. "I observed your show with the giant little prince, even if I were to lend you my great strength I'm not sure it would not be enough to move either of the great stones, let alone both.

"I agree, but I've another plan," said Jahmo, "call three of your strongest brothers to aid us if you will quickly."

The elephant obeyed. Two of the elephants pushed one stone while the other two pushed the remaining one. Together the might beasts had the huge rocks rolling around the mountain. "Remember my friends," Jahmo said, as he rode the back of the first bull elephant, "keep your selves hidden behind the stones, that giant must not see you." "Yes little prince," they replied.

The Giant had nearly completed his task, he was already on the other side of the mountain puffing and grunting leaning into the mighty stone. His strength was now all gone, when, he saw the two great stones thundering toward him throwing dust into the air, crashing through the brush, rumbling like two giant eggs, then stopping right in front of him.

When Little Jahmo stepped from behind them, slapping his hands together dusting them off, Booli's eyes bulged, popping with disbelief for the first time ever, he felt helpless and very small. Jahmo wasn't even sweating or breathing hard he didn't seem tired at all. The Giant was powerless while the little Prince was full of energy.

It appears I gave you too much of an advantage Giant, you made it here first," Jahmo said. "That makes me very angry," Jahmo said with a cold look in his eye. "I demand satisfaction," he snarled winking at the four elephants hiding behind the hug stones. "All right Giant, it's time!" he roared, "It's time for the games to end!" Jahmo started toward the Giant sternly. Booli was still in shock over the little Prince's mighty feat and how effortlessly he'd performed it.

Jahmo continued slowly toward the Giant, gritting his teeth, his fists clenched tightly. "Now, I'm going to grind your over grown carcass into the dust, now, I'm going to rend you limb from limb. Booli found himself flinching at the Little Prince's words and wondering if he was actually as powerful as he seemed to be. "Now Booli!" said Jahmo. The Giant suddenly found himself quaking in fear his hand over his mouth as he

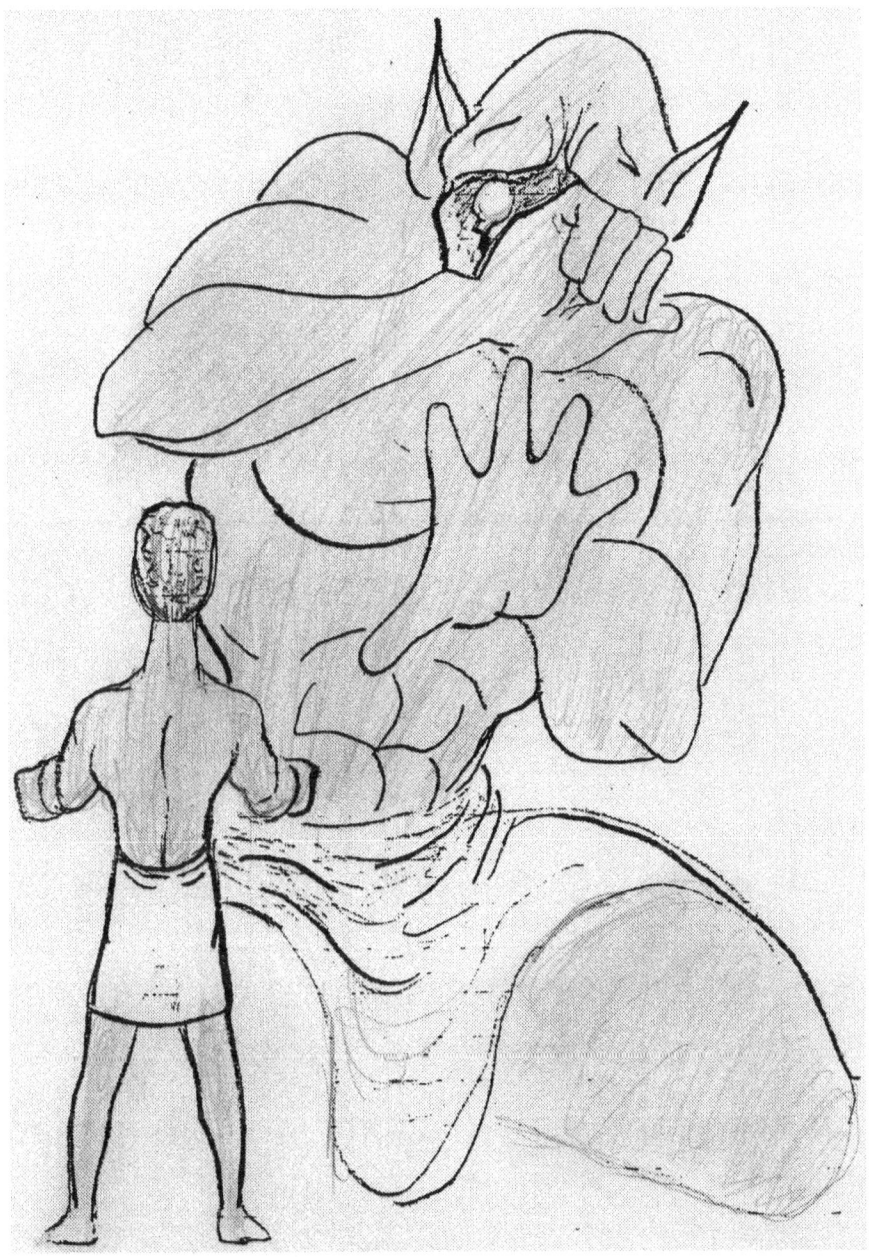

gasped for breath. The thought of having his bones snapped was a little unsettling.

"Now Giant!" Jahmo screamed raising his fist as though to strike. "NO! Please NO!" the Giant shrieked. Falling to his knees, "Don't hurt me mighty Prince spare me," he cried, his eyes beginning to water. "I'll mend my wicked ways mighty Prince I swear it, just spare my wretched life!"

Jahmo stood silent for a long moment

as the Giant cowered before him,

"Very well Giant I will spare you this

day." "You will leave this land."

"Yes, yes I am leaving," the Giant

said rising to his feet. "I am not

finished!" Jahmo shouted. The Giant

sat back down timidly. "I am going to

hold you to your vow to mend your

131

ways." "You will not return to this land, but if I even hear of you plaguing anyone else anywhere I will come for you, and you will not be as fortunate as today." "And remember Giant I will know if you go back on your word." "Yes Great Prince," the Giant said humbly, "I will not forget, I will never forget." The Giant rose and ran off.

The Giant was never seen again, but word often came from far off travelers of how a gentle friendly Giant helped them and their people. Harvesting whole fields in a day, digging deep wells in mere moments. Prince Jahmo always smiled when he heard of the good deeds Booli performed and took a special pride in them himself.

TOMU AND JAHMO

He and the Princess were wed and

he was a wise and kind king. He and

Queen Tomu had a tall handsome son with special gifts himself. Their son always smiled when he'd see his parents looking into each other's eyes.

www.ingramcontent.com/pod-product-compliance
Lightning Source LLC
Chambersburg PA
CBHW051421280526
45785CB00003B/1114